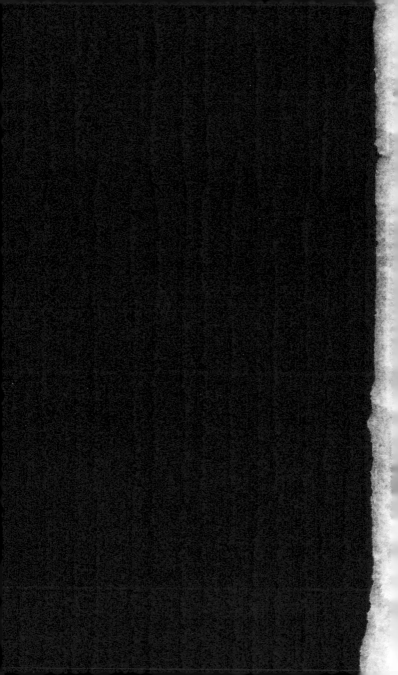

MANIFESTOS FOR THE 21ST CENTURY

SERIES EDITORS: URSULA OWEN AND JUDITH VIDAL-HALL

Free expression is as high on the agenda as it
has ever been, though not always for the
happiest of reasons. Here, distinguished writers
address the issue of censorship in a
complex and fragile world where people with
widely different cultural habits and beliefs are
living in close proximity, where offence is easily
taken, and where words, images and behaviour
are coming under the closest scrutiny.
These books will surprise, clarify and provoke
in equal measure.

Index on Censorship is the only international
magazine promoting and protecting free
expression. A haven for the censored and
silenced, it has built an impressive track record
since it was founded 35 years ago, publishing
some of the finest writers, sharpest analysts and
foremost thinkers in the world. In this series
with Seagull Books, the focus will be on
questions of rights, liberties, tolerance,
silencing, censorship and dissent.

OFFENCE
the hindu case

SALIL TRIPATHI

LONDON NEW YORK CALCUTTA

Seagull Books 2009

© Salil Tripathi 2009

ISBN-13   978 1 90649 738 5

British Library Cataloguing-in-Publication Data
A catalogue record for this book is available
from the British Library

Typeset and designed by Seagull Books, Calcutta, India
Printed in Calcutta at Rockwel Offset

For Harsha Tripathi
(1935–2004)

My Mother's Fault

You marched with other seven-year-
    old girls,
Singing songs of freedom at dawn in rural
    Gujarat,
Believing that would shame the British and
    they would leave India.

Five years later, they did.

You smiled,
When you first saw Maqbool Fida Husain's
    nude sketches of Hindu goddesses,

And laughed,
When I told you that some people wanted
    to burn his art.

'Have those people seen any of our ancient
    sculptures? Those are far naughtier,'
You said.

Your voice broke,
On December 6, 1992,
As you called me at my office in Singapore,
When they destroyed the Babri Masjid.

'We have just killed Gandhi again,' you said.

We had.

Aavu te karaay koi divas? (Can anyone do
    such a thing any time?)
You asked, aghast,
Staring at the television,
As Hindu mobs went, house-to-house,
Looking for Muslims to kill,
After a train compartment in Godhra burned,
Killing 58 Hindus in February 2002.

You were right, each time.

After reading what I've been writing over
     the years,
Some folks have complained that I just
     don't get it.

I live abroad: what do I know of India?

But I knew you; that was enough.

And that's why I turned out this way.

CONTENTS

ACKNOWLEDGEMENTS

A book such as this would not have been possible but for the wisdom, friendship, co-operation and support from many individuals. I'd like to thank my editors at various publications over the years, who let me have my say on free speech, at *India Today, Mint, Tehelka, Far Eastern Economic Review, Celebrity* and *The Indian Post in Asia*; *The International Herald Tribune, Index on Censorship, The New Statesman* and *The Spectator* in Europe; and *The Wall Street Journal, Salon* and *The Washington Post* in the United States.

I would also like to thank Amit Varma, Arshia Sattar, Aamer Hussein, Susie Thomas and Rohit Chopra for commenting on early drafts of the manuscript; Rita Banerji, B. R. Mani and Romila Thapar for explaining to me aspects of India's past; and Nikhil Mehra, Shruti Rajagopalan and Gautam Patel, for discussing with me India's censorship laws. The errors are all mine; the added wisdom, theirs.

Finally, I thank my sons, Udayan and Ameya: may they live in a world where nobody tells them what they must, or cannot, read, watch or listen.

IN THE BEGINNING . . .

On a warm summer evening in 2008, the Indian capital New Delhi held the Indian Art Summit, the nation's first art fair, which included a sculpture park, art films, specially curated projects and the works by 300 of India's finest artists. The auction house Sotheby's and the Indian government supported it.

One painter was absent—Maqbool Fida Husain, easily India's greatest living artist. Flamboyant and controversial, Husain is the mascot of post-Independence Indian art, famous not only for his paintings, through which he has chronicled modern India, but also for his acute sense, combining Dali-like flair for exhibitionism with Picasso's genius for commerce: he realized the value of his signature early in his career and, in the process, made Indian art a worthwhile investment. Today, some of his works fetch nearly a million dollars.

Husain started his life painting Bollywood billboards. Those garish images of larger-than-life stars staring down traffic at busy signals shaped his choice of colours, sense of drama and design. Later, he turned to creative work. Inspired by German Expressionism, Husain has stayed in the limelight, not only through his elegant rendering of horses—a lifetime obsession—but also by capturing the nation's zeitgeist over the past six decades and becoming the artistic equivalent of India's poet laureate: celebrating the nation's triumphs—from

cricket stars like Sachin Tendulkar to Bollywood actresses like Madhuri Dixit—and
weeping over its tragedies—from assassina-
tions to natural disasters. All along, he has
celebrated India's diversity, embodying its
syncretic and inclusive culture.

Yet, for over a decade now, Husain has
been forced to spend long periods in
exile—in Dubai during winter, in London
during warmer times. He has told journalists he would love to return to the city he
calls his first home—Bombay—but Hindu
nationalists have waged a successful campaign against his art. They are offended
because he paints Hindu deities in the
nude. And organizers of art exhibitions are
increasingly wary of displaying his works or
mentioning him in a catalogue.

To understand why, let us take our story
to a cool December evening in 1996, at Sir
Cowasji Jehangir Hall, lit up as if it were
India's Independence Day, in downtown

Bombay. India's finest painters, liveliest art critics and trendiest socialites are inside, mingling with art collectors and the state's governor, marking the transformation of the venerable building into the city's first world-class art museum, as it becomes the additional wing of the National Gallery of Modern Art in New Delhi.

Appropriately enough, the inaugural show is dedicated to the Progressive Artists Group, a remarkable movement founded in 1948 by six painters and sculptors—besides Husain, Syed Haider Raza, Francis Newton Souza, Hari Ambadas Gade, Krishna Howalji Ara and Sadanand Bakre—who had set out to create a new Indian artistic idiom. Their inspiration was drawn from eclectic sources, Indian traditions as well as Western modernity, and they helped solidify the secular, liberal, urbane, cosmopolitan and modern ethos of India.

India's independence had been a violent affair: the Partition of the country in 1947 into India and Pakistan had caused brutal upheavals and massacres,[1] convulsing the land and irrigating the fields of Punjab and Bengal with rivers of blood. While never characterized as genocide, credible estimates suggest that nearly 17 million people were displaced and some 3 million remain unaccounted for, many of them dying in sectarian violence.

While politics and religion divided the people, many Indians were inspired by the ethos of inclusive secularism in which all faiths were equal. That was also the governing philosophy of India's founding fathers, the ascetic leader Mohandas Karamchand Gandhi and the first Prime Minister, the Cambridge-educated Jawaharlal Nehru.

In the years since, India's record in maintaining a secular order as well as protecting minorities has been poor.

Thousands have died in communal riots and discrimination remains prevalent. At the same time, at an individual level, many minorities—Muslims, Christians, Sikhs, Jains and Zoroastrians—have thrived. But in that first flush of Independence, the Indian mood was inspired; the Progressive Artists wanted to capture that and, in their own way, they made that enthusiasm the heartbeat of the new India.

That night in 1996 at the Cowasji Jehangir Hall was meant to celebrate that same enthusiasm. The city needed the healing art can provide. The gallery was opening three years after communal riots devoured the city. Those riots were unusual for Bombay. As a commercially-driven port city, Bombay thrives on trade and exchange, and its traders are largely unconcerned about each other's caste, creed, faith or language. But this cohesion tore apart in early 1993 after a series of coordinated bomb blasts destroyed several key buildings, including the city's passport office and the Air India building, killing 257 people. This was in retaliation for the destruction of Babri Masjid by a Hindu mob in December 1992, brainwashed into believing that the sixteenth-century mosque stood on the site of an ancient temple commemorating the precise birth spot of Rama, an icon from the Hindu pantheon.

As India's most cosmopolitan city, with no language group enjoying a clear majority, Bombay has usually stayed away from such violence. At its best, it personifies what a united India is capable of. In his 1995 novel, *The Moor's Last Sigh*,[2] Bombay-born novelist Salman Rushdie observes: 'Those who hated India, those who sought to ruin it, would need to ruin Bombay.' Rushdie's novel went on to condemn the bomb blasts later, saying: 'O Bombay . . . You were the glory of your time. But a darker time came

upon you . . . For the barbarians were not
only at our gates, but within our skins. We
were our own wooden horses, each one of
us full of our doom. We were both the
bombers and the bombs.'[3]

Officially, by 1996, Bombay had already
ceased to be Bombay: a regional political
party, the Shiv Sena, had campaigned for
years to change its name to Mumbai, arguing for its 'real' name derived from Mum-
badevi, a local goddess. In 1995, the federal
government obliged. There has been some
argument that Bombay owes its origin to
the Portuguese phrase, Bom Bahia,[4] or 'a
good bay', but the Shiv Sena is not a party
to welcome an academic discourse, as many
artists, academics and dissenters have
found out over the years, many preferring
silence and acquiescence. The process of
attacking and renaming what they do not
approve of in the name of Hindu religion
has been the way of Shiv Sena activists for

some time now. Their most visible target that night in 1996 was Husain.

Husain stayed away from the party—had he come, he would have been arrested. Bombay was no longer the warm welcoming hometown Husain knew; he could not live there safely, nor visit. That evening, at the Cowasji Jehangir Hall, a group of young artists unfurled a banner which read: 'Husain, we miss you.' As the night lengthened, getting chillier by Bombay's warm standards, and women wrapped themselves in shawls and men who had worn jackets felt they had made a wise choice, the conversation grew heated. A well-known Western collector of Indian art was incensed that nobody had spoken out for Husain, and asked loudly why the city's intellectuals were not defending Husain more passionately. An old friend, married to a painter, asked me in turn, 'Why doesn't he understand? This is like asking us to speak out in Berlin in 1936.'

Husain's sketch of Saraswati.

In September 1996, an old sketch of Husain's, of a nude Saraswati, Goddess of Learning, had surfaced when the Hindi magazine *Vichar Mimansa* (Discussion of Thoughts) published an article about this controversial work. The controversy spread across India, as eight individuals from different parts of the country filed criminal complaints against him, saying his art offended their religious sensibilities. Could you really show a goddess without clothes? The Shiv Sena protested, as did the Bharatiya Janata Party (BJP), the national opposition in parliament. The police immediately decided to arrest Husain for disturbing communal harmony.

In his 2008 film *Rang Rasiya* (Colours of Passion), Ketan Mehta shows us a similar controversy that almost ended the career of Raja Ravi Varma, the painter whose images of Hindu divinities now adorn most calendars in India. His pictures of a partly clothed woman had caused an uproar in early-twentieth-century India, and Hindu nationalists then had sued him for obscenity. At the screening of his film at the London International Film Festival in October 2008, Mehta said: 'The persecution of artists today is a continuation of intolerance that is at least a century old.'

Neither lascivious nor derisive, Husain's sketch of Saraswati had stirred admiration. But times had changed. A militant brand of Hinduism, *Hindutva* (Hindu-ness), had emerged, arguing that the government's secular policies were an excuse to appease minorities and that Hindu identity was being insulted. Some Hindu activists asked: 'Why does he paint only Hindu goddesses in the nude, and not Ayesha, Prophet Mohammed's wife?' Typical was an Internet post from a concerned Hindu-American: 'Husain is a Muslim by faith. What on earth prompts him to choose only

Hindu Gods and Goddesses for such dis-
graceful and ridiculous portrayal? He has
mistaken Hindus' tolerance for their weak-
nesses.'

Acting on such sentiments, Hindu nationalists took the law into their hands. In
October that year, a Hindu mob ransacked
a private art gallery in Ahmedabad, where a
major retrospective of Husain's works was
planned. Ironically, while the police in
Bombay were prompt in issuing an arrest
warrant against Husain, to this day nobody
has been charged for destroying his work in
Ahmedabad.

For the first 40 years of India's independence, Hindu nationalist voices were
isolated and marginal in the Indian political spectrum. But, since the mid-1980s, for
reasons we shall see later, they have grown
more vocal and aggressive. By the mid-
1990s, the single-largest political party in
Parliament was the BJP, the latest incarna-

tion of the Bharatiya Jana Sangh, the political arm of the Rashtriya Swayamsevak Sangh (RSS), a Hindu nationalist organization partly inspired by European fascism and Nazism. In 1996, following the Congress Party's defeat in parliamentary elections, the BJP even led a coalition government that lasted 13 days, before making way for a short-lived left-leaning alliance. The BJP finally came to power as the head of the National Democratic Alliance and ruled India between 1998 and 2004.

While the BJP professed to play by parliamentary rules, several of its allies—in particular the Shiv Sena in Maharashtra—often used force. The Shiv Sena had risen into prominence by targeting 'outsiders'—those who came to Bombay and ostensibly took away jobs from the local, Marathi-speaking population. Once it had secured a footing in Bombay, it sought expansion in the state and decided to transfer its chauvinism from language to religion. Outside Bombay, Marathi was pretty much the *lingua franca*, and linguistic chauvinism, relevant to whip up support in Bombay, had little value in Maharashtra's hinterland. By the mid-1990s, the Shiv Sena ran a coalition government with the BJP in the state.

THE LETTER AND THE SPIRIT

Major religions not only emerge from myths that reinforce the message that good ultimately triumphs over evil, they also create their own myths to describe and justify their beliefs. But acts of unparalleled cruelty have been committed in the name of each such religion: the Christian inquisitions, the suicide bombings of Islamic terrorists, the false piety of Burmese generals who claim to be Buddhists and the Hindu nationalists' attacks on minorities, particularly Muslims,

are only some of many examples of the evil
that men and women of God do.

Hinduism is often described not as a religion but as a 'way of life', or as the life of
dharma, a set of beliefs and practices with a
fairly liberal range of acceptable behaviour.
Hinduism has room for those who believe
in all the thousands of gods as well as for
those who believe in none. It has a 'neither-
this-nor-that' quality that seeks to remind
the believer of the complexity of life, drawing him away from the Manichean divides
that force people to choose between this
and that. Hinduism does not have one
prophet, nor does it have one book, and it
certainly does not have one shrine considered holier than all the others and where
the faithful must go at least once in their
lives. This does not make Jerusalem, the
Vatican or Mecca any less important but it
does show where some Hindu ideas—unity
in diversity, tolerance, acceptance of fate—

come from. At one level, anything goes in Hinduism, because everything is possible and it is not for the human to divine good and bad. In the great epic Mahabharata, forces of good act in ways that may seem conniving and unethical but they do so in order that truth may eventually succeed over lies and good over evil. Books like the four Vedas, Upanishads and the *Bhagavad-gita*—the *shastra*s, or scriptures—provide a broad range of rules to guide the Hindu towards the right path.[5]

And because no one individual controls the eternal truth, every view, in theory, is acceptable. So you can cover up your goddess in the finest silk and jewellery. Or you can watch her naked. You can look at the beauty of her face and admire the divinity of her halo, a sari wrapped around her and her face made up like a Bollywood queen. Or you can see her with her ample breasts heaving, her luscious lips parted seduc-

Erotic details from the Lakshmana temple, Khajuraho.

tively, her thighs wrapped in supreme sexual ecstasy around an athletic god—or even
goddess—carved for eternity on the walls of
a Hindu temple. The relationship between
the goddess and the devotee is an individual one; there aren't supposed to be inter-
mediaries interfering with how the devotee
should interpret her. At least, that's the theory and it's been the practice in large parts
of India for thousands of years.

But Hindu nationalists have a different
project in mind. Grown intolerant of views
and representations they disagree with, they
have attacked painters, ransacked art galleries, destroyed research institutes, insulted academics, challenged history, had
books withdrawn, extracted apologies from
Hollywood stars and studios, destroyed a
mosque and killed and raped many Muslims. And they are able to get away with
their calls for bans because India's Constitution does not offer First Amendment-type

guarantees for free speech and expression. Under Article 19(1)(a), all citizens have the right to 'freedom of speech and expression'—but there are 'reasonable restrictions' on the right, which permit the state to restrict it 'in the interests of the sovereignty and integrity of India, the security of the State, friendly relations with foreign States, public order, decency or morality, or in relation to contempt of court, defamation or incitement to an offence'.

Then there is Section 295(A) of the Indian Penal Code, which makes it a criminal act to 'outrage religious feelings' with malicious intent. Another section, 153(A) outlaws 'promoting enmity between different groups on grounds of religion, race, place of birth, residence, language, etc. and doing acts prejudicial to maintenance of harmony'. These clauses provide the basis for busybodies with time on their hands to sue writers, artists, actors, filmmakers and

other public personalities for expressing
themselves in ways that offend them.

India's censorious record is long. It
banned D. H. Lawrence's novel, *Lady Chat-
terley's Lover* in 1964,[6] a full five years after
the UK lifted its ban on the novel, and it
has the dubious honour of being the first
country in the world to ban Salman
Rushdie's *The Satanic Verses*. Following public protests the Maharashtra Government
banned *Riddles of Hinduism* by Bhimrao
Ambedkar, a lawyer who came from the for-
merly 'untouchable' Mahar community and
who is regarded as the architect of India's
Constitution; but following counter-
protests, it reinstated the book, with a
caveat saying the Government did not agree
with certain specific views of Ambedkar.[7] C.
Aubrey Menen's telling of the Ramayana is
banned too. Over the years, fearing public
unrest, the Indian state has often caved in
to demands by banning works of art even

before a formal case is filed, merely because an interest group claims its feelings are being offended. The state takes the easier option of banning the work rather than promoting a liberal environment in which a more enlightened discourse may be possible.

Taking advantage of the state's weakness, Hindu activists, for much of the past decade, have attacked artists, writers, historians and academics they do not like or disagree with. They have destroyed Husain's paintings whenever they have had the opportunity, picketed art galleries, protested against television shows they consider immoral, and objected to films that depict history in ways that are contrary to their opinions of it. Taking its cue from this sort of behaviour, state governments have banned films that may offend particular communities within the Hindu faith.

In early 2009, the Goa unit of the Hindu Janjagruti Samiti (Hindu People's

Awakening Committee) sought a ban on the
Oscar winner *Slumdog Millionaire,* because
the scene of a Hindu–Muslim riot showed a
boy dressed as Rama looking in a sinister
way at the protagonist children (who are
Muslims) fleeing the violence, and because
a Hindu girl fell in love with a Muslim boy.
In late 2007, the governments of Uttar
Pradesh and Punjab banned a film called
Aaja Naach Le (Let's Dance), the comeback
vehicle of Madhuri Dixit, on the grounds
that the song, *'Bole mochi bhi khud ko sonar
hai'* (The cobbler thinks he is a goldsmith)
implied that the cobbler caste was socially
inferior to the goldsmith and was, therefore,
implicitly derogatory because it created a
hierarchy perpetuating discrimination
against lower, socially disadvantaged castes.
In several parts of the country, distributors
could not release another film, *Jodhaa Akbar,*
a fictionalized account of the Mughal king,
because the Rajput community was offended

over some historical inaccuracies. Four
northern states—Uttar Pradesh, Rajasthan,
Haryana and Uttarakhand—banned the
film, although the Supreme Court allowed
its release later. To be fair, the governments
that have imposed some of these bans are
not necessarily run by Hindu nationalists;
in fact, the Uttar Pradesh government is
run by Mayawati, a woman from the dalit
community, as the underprivileged classes
at the bottom of Hinduism's complex caste
hierarchy are known.

Taking their battle to the new generation, Hindu nationalists have objected to
urban teenagers exchanging Valentine's
Day cards on the grounds that (as well as
being against the Hindu ethos) it is a
'Christian' custom and promotes romance
between young people. A group in Karnataka stormed pubs in Bangalore, arguing
that they were against local customs and
sought restrictions on pubs. Dancing in

pubs is now not allowed in the city. And, in January 2009, another Hindu group, Sri Rama Sene (Lord Rama's Army), not only attacked a pub in Mangalore but also assaulted several young women inside who were enjoying their drink and abducted a couple because the young man and woman were not from the same religion.

As for Husain himself, when NDTV, an Indian television network, asked its viewers to poll on the question 'Should Husain be given the Bharat Ratna?' (India's highest civilian honour), Hindu youths from the Hindu Samrajya Sena (Army of the Hindu Empire), stormed the studio in Gujarat, damaging property and attacking employees. At one point, about 1,200 cases were pending against Husain in various courts in India.

Courts have risen to the occasion. In May 2008, Justice Sanjay Kishan Kaul issued a ringing judgement in three such

cases, dismissing the concerns of the 'puri-
tanists' after finding them to be 'baseless':

> In a free and democratic society, toler-
> ance is vital. It is very unfortunate that
> the works of any artists today who have
> tried to play around with nudity have
> come under scrutiny. These artists have
> had to face the music, making them
> think twice before exhibiting their work
> of art . . . We have been called the land of
> the *Kama Sutra*, then why is it that in the
> land of *Kama Sutra* we shy away from its
> very name? Beauty lies in the eyes of the
> beholder and so does obscenity.[8]

He condemned those who criticize
Husain as 'the types who would not go to
art galleries or have interest in contemporary art . . . because if they did, they would
know that there are many artists who
embrace nudity as part of contemporary
art,' and concluded:

> India's new 'puritanism', practised by a
> largely ignorant crowd in the name of

Indian spiritual purity, is threatening to throw the nation back into the Pre-Renaissance era. Criminal justice system should not be used as an easy recourse to ventilate against a creative act. Each painting has a story to narrate. Art to every artist is a vehicle for personal expression. In fact, he (Husain) had consistently maintained that he actually celebrates nudity and considered it as the purest form of expression. The test for judging a work of art should be that of an ordinary man of common sense and not that of a hypersensitive one . . . Our greatest problem today is fundamentalism, the triumph of the letter over the spirit.[9]

While a senior Indian law official immediately added that his government would ask the law commission to clarify measures to protect artists, it is not yet clear if the verdict can dismiss other pending cases against Husain. Indeed, despite a September 2008 verdict by the Supreme Court dismissing five different cases against

Bharat Mata *by M. F. Husain.*

him for depicting *Bharat Mata*, or Mother India, in the nude, lawyers say it is still not clear if he can return to India without being threatened with an arrest.

The attacks are not restricted to Husain. Fearing public unrest, a few years ago, Bombay's police officials visited an exhibition of figurative drawings of renowned painter Jatin Das and advised him to post a notice saying the paintings were suitable only for those over 18. And on 9 May 2007, a Hindu nationalist group stormed into the Maharaja Sayajirao University campus, Baroda, in western India and assaulted an award-winning art student named Chandramohan Srimantula. Like Husain, his work includes nude Hindu deities as well as a painting depicting the crucifix. For good measure, the Hindu activists brought along a few Christians as well. They roughed up the art student and had him arrested by the local police; the following day, a judge sent him to the city's central jail.

While the university's dean supported Chandramohan, the administrators, in an act of stunning cowardice, refused to post bail or offer any legal help; instead, they asked him to apologize. When the charges focused on the courageous dean as well, the university refused to support him either. Not only was this a blow to free expression and academic freedom, on the face of it the arrest was illegal. Leading artists and writers from around India protested and Chandramohan was finally released on bail, on condition that he notify the police if he planned to leave the state or the country while the case was pending.

HOW TO GET THINGS WRONG
WITHOUT EVEN TRYING

Near the end of James Joyce's *A Portrait of the Artist as a Young Man* (1916), Stephen Dedalus tells the reader:

I will not serve that in which I no longer
believe, whether it call itself my home,
my fatherland, or my church: and I will
try to express myself in some mode of
life or art as freely as I can and as wholly
as I can, using for my defence the only
arms I allow myself to use—silence, exile
and cunning.[10]

For Husain, these words now carry a
special meaning: opposition to him and
his work has now travelled beyond India's
borders. In 2006, a group of Hindu activists
attacked two of his paintings at an upscale
art gallery, asserting that if Muslims could
ban cartoons of Prophet Mohammed made
by Danish artists, why couldn't Hindus do
the same with Husain's art? What was unusual about this act of vandalism was that
the gallery was in central London, at Asia
House near Oxford Circus.

Ironically, even as various police officers in India were issuing arrest warrants

against Husain, the then Indian High Commissioner in London, Kamalesh Sharma, was inaugurating the show, where he called Husain India's 'greatest modern artist' and added, 'Husain's career and success mirrors closely the meteoric rise of contemporary Indian art on the international stage.'

Indeed, if Indian art today commands good prices at international auctions, the credit for that goes to artists such as Husain, Tyeb Mehta and the late Amrita Sher-Gil. Noting these trends in the art market, Suneet Chopra noted in *The Financial Express*:

> Husain's Gupta-style figuration can clothe a minor film personality like Madhuri Dixit with the eternal aura of a *Gajagamini*[11] or create forms of goddesses easy to reach out to and touch, humanising them as pre-Hindutva Hinduism would want to. His Kunti is not a dull

matriarch but a Nair princess without many lovers helping her to bear a brood of many fathers but only one mother. To see Kunti in any other light would kill the *Mahabharata* and reduce it to hypocritical text celebrating war. Husain has saved our epics from being drowned in reverential formaldehyde. He has given them life. Condemn him and you are condemning a market that more than doubles itself in value every year because it visually stimulates thoughts. Collectors appreciate that and it is evident that despite the hysterical attacks on Husain, his works are over half in value all sales in our contemporary markets. From this perspective one realises that the nude in art can equally be the self or the ideal other as in the case of the Jain Tirthankara images. So it would appear to be a gross perversity to persecute Husain for something our tradition clearly shows is not lewd. Also, attempts to limit our tradition to very narrow forms of expression will impoverish it and end the richness that has given it importance in the world.[12]

At the heart of the activists' complaints against Husain's art is that he paints Hindu deities—Monkey-God Hanuman, the elephant-headed Ganesha, Rama's consort Sita; Goddess of Learning, Saraswati—without clothes. Such a complaint could have merit, at least on cultural grounds, if nudity were an alien concept in Hindu art. But Husain is hardly a pioneer here; for millennia, Hindu divinities have appeared unclothed in art. When Husain depicts a Hindu deity in the nude, he is following an aspect of Hindu, or Indic, tradition; he is not insulting it or defying it. By challenging his art and attacking him, his critics are going against the grain of Hindu tradition; they are acting as Hinduism's moral Taliban.

Since the late 1980s, Hindu nationalists have been successful in convincing a sizeable proportion of Hindus that they are the vic-

tims of a form of reverse discrimination.
Muslims, they argue, are undeserving
recipients of benefits from the state. For this
appeasement of minorities, the BJP blames
the Congress, which ruled India uninter-
rupted from 1947 to 1977 and since then
from 1980 to 1989, from 1991 to 1996 and
in a coalition from 2004. The BJP's slogan is
'equality for all, appeasement to none',
which sounds attractive to many. If Muslims
can get *The Satanic Verses* banned in India, if
they can gain exemption from a common
civil code applicable to all Indians, if their
pilgrims get subsidies to go on Haj—a privi-
lege denied to poor Hindus who may want
to go on pilgrimages too—then something is
rotten in the state of India, or so runs the
reasoning.

In such a climate, it may seem naïve for
painters like Husain or Chandramohan to
paint Hindu deities in the nude and assume
they can get away with it.

But the corollary of Justice Kaul's reasoning is that vulgarity lies in the eye of the beholder. Husain's paintings aren't meant to titillate; these are not classic, voluptuous human forms in the conventional Western sense, drawn realistically in identifiable settings. Rather, they elevate the body to an abstract realm, suggesting the formlessness of divinity. Hinduism has a concept, *nirakara*, describing just that. Such an explanation, however, is too abstract for the fundamentalists. Husain understands that and has apologized to those whose sentiments are hurt. Explaining his motives, he traced his art to India's millennia-old heritage, where gods and goddesses are 'pure and uncovered', as he puts it. Indian painters, he adds, are the 'direct descendants of that golden era . . . of great vision that transcends the mundane reality' where the human form turns into a metaphorical structure. 'My work goes beyond reality; it does not recreate reality,' he says.[13]

That a Muslim artist in Hindu-dominated India can paint Hindu deities freely is something to celebrate. Not only does it show the high degree of artistic freedom in India, and its composite ethos, but it also projects India's liberalism at its best. As a recent exhibition of the Ramayana at the British Library showed, manuscripts were often painted for Hindu kings by Muslim artists. Muslim classical singers in India have routinely sung divine songs invoking Hindu gods.

But some Hindus are seething over a peculiar injustice: Muslims command the world's attention when they are offended by images they consider blasphemous—a concept alien in Hinduism—and they now want equal treatment. That is, they want the right to be offended. What these activists forget is that the sacred and the profane have always coexisted in India. India gave the world *Kama Sutra* and millions of Hindus worship

Woodcut depicting Lord Krishna stealing the gopinis' *clothes.*

Shiva's *linga*, or the phallus. As a faith, Hinduism is broad enough to include some sects that think that sex is the primary way to attain enlightenment, and understands that some ascetics are preaching abstinence when they roam around naked, their bodies smeared with ash, during major religious congregations.

Architects have decorated the walls and pillars of some Hindu temples with nude deities. Walking through a temple, you might get the impression that Hindus take their idols lightly. Here, a god is stealing the clothes of damsels frolicking in a lake; there, another encouraging his brother to cut off the nose and ears of an admirer. On many walls of great temples, minor gods and goddesses engage in sexual acts that would never be shown on television before the threshold hour.

Erotic art was the hallmark of the temple architecture of the Chandela dynasty

for a good reason. As B. R. Mani, Joint
Director-General, Archaeological Survey of
India, explains:

> The erotic scenes were placed only on
> the outer surface of the temples as they
> depicted playful life of human nature.
> The structure of the temple represents
> the body of *purusha* (man). The three
> primordial elements, or *gunas,* are em-
> bodied in the structure, and the worship-
> per, after looking at it and realising these
> elements of human nature, embellished
> on the outer walls, enters in the temple
> where all these elements disappear, or
> rather merge into the great feeling of
> spiritual bliss and nearness to the God.[14]

Hindu iconography reveals this in a
startling way. Think of the sensuousness of
an almost nude Parvati (Shiva's wife) in the
eleventh-century Brihadeeshwara temple at
Gangaikondacholapuram: it does not in
any way diminish her holiness. Bronze
sculptures of scantily clad Hindu goddesses

Shiva and Parvati. Detail, Brihadeeshwara temple, Gangaikondacholapuram.

made during the Chola period (ninth to thirteenth century) are no less divine. The temples in Khajuraho from the Chandela period have hundreds of erotic statues and idols. And a marble Jain statue at Pallu, Bikaner (from the Solanki period, *c*.1200) has a nude Saraswati, clad only in exquisite and ornate chains, necklaces and bangles.

While it is true that temples built since the Islamic invasions began do not have explicit art on their walls, the reasons for that are complex. Some critics have blamed Muslim invaders for destroying temples because they were against idol worship. Others have cited the strict rules imposed by Victorian morality[15] after British rule began in India. One explanation may be the decline in royal patronage: As Mani explains, 'The disappearance of erotic art is not directly connected with Islamic attacks, though the construction of new ones came to a halt in the magnitude in which it took place in the pre-Islamic days.'[16]

Art historian Rita Banerji suggests that a good section of British and most Muslim colonizers found the sexual sensibilities and ways of Indians to be unappealing and un-aesthetic, besides appearing to be immoral. Pointing out the difference in the general perception towards sex and sensuality between AD 200–1100 and the colonial period that follows, Banerji explains:

> There was an open, almost celebratory eroticism (in the earlier period) to just about everything: art, music, dance, literature, philosophy, religion and regular norms and customs. Underlying it all was a basic philosophy that established a connection between sex, sexuality and the Divine—not only the Tantra cults, but the others too—the Shaktas, the Shaivites, the Vaishnavas. Even among the Buddhists and Jains—tantric cults emerged in this period. And in temples where there was no overt practise of sex and sensuality—they would use the *karavira* and the *aparajita* flowers,

(representing the phallus and vagina re-
spectively) in worship to symbolize
coition. The basic change in the colonial
period lay in the disassociation of sex
and the sacred, through the religions of
the colonizers.[17]

After the Muslim occupation of northern India, erotic temples and worship
emerged in areas that the Muslims did not
occupy or that held out against occupation
for a long time, such as Hampi and the
Kamakhya temple in Assam. Areas of India
with minimal contact with Muslim rule also
did not see women adopting the veil. Many
Muslim rulers adopted the *shariah* in the
parts of India they ruled, even though they
were privately self-indulgent, and imposed
censorship on Hindu literature, arts and
poetry of this period. The British took that
much further, banning books, sanitizing
scriptures, branding as obscene certain
forms of theatre, even sending the police to
stop performances.

In other words, the behaviour of today's Hindu nationalists mirrors the behaviour of the colonizers, and not a continuing tradition; if anything, it is Husain, and other artists, who are the true inheritors of that tradition.

Indeed, the hypocrisy of Husain's critics is clear when one notices that, while Hindu activists in London attacked Asia House when it showed Husain's art, they were absent when London's Underground network carried large images of a Hindu deity, looking sinuous and sensual, cavorting cheerfully and wearing almost nothing, advertising an exhibition of Chola bronzes at the Royal Academy of Arts. Nearly 2.5 million commuters saw the naked god daily, but no Hindu objected.

Unlike Husain, the artists who made those sculptures were unknown, though assumed to be Hindu; again, unlike Husain's almost-abstract drawings, the Chola

Parvati. Chola bronze. Photograph by Robert Nash.

bronzes are curvaceous and vivacious, leav-
ing little to the imagination. It is clear that
what runs against the Indian ethos is not
Husain's art but the activists' fury. While
what Husain paints may not be sacred, what
the fanatics are doing is profane.

FIGHTING FOR THE SOUL OF RAMA

> The curious fact is that as we move into
> the 21st century, historians have become
> central to politics. We historians are the
> monopoly suppliers of the past. The only
> way to modify the past that does not
> sooner or later go through historians is by
> destroying the past. Mythology is taking
> over from knowledge.[18]

If history represents collective memory, and
if it is to be objective and not written by
victors, it becomes important to guard its
sanctity. After the artists, the Hindu nationalists' prime target is Indian history. In late

February 2008, a group of Hindus stormed into the History Department of the University of Delhi, breaking windows and causing general mayhem. They belonged to the Akhil Bharatiya Vidyarthi Parishad (All India Students' Council), the student wing of the BJP. They were angry because the professors had directed students to read an essay on the Ramayana that they considered 'blasphemous'.

The essay, 'Three Hundred Ramayanas: Five Examples and Three Thoughts on Translation',[19] by the distinguished poet A. K. Ramanujan, a Macarthur Genius Fellow who died in 1993 in the US where he taught at the University of Chicago, marvels at the sheer diversity and range of the epic Ramayana, and recounts many of the unusual and alternate renderings of the myth, pointing out the vibrant plurality in religion and literature. The head of the History Department, a quiet academic called Saiyid Zaheer Hussain Jafri, is, as his name suggests, a Muslim. The professor who assigned the essay is Upinder Singh, who happens to be Sikh and the daughter of India's Prime Minister Manmohan Singh. This particular combination gave the nationalists further ammunition.

The conventional Ramayana narrative is complicated enough.[20] Most interpretations tell a story with which many Indians, Hindu or not, are familiar. But as you travel through the length and breadth of the vast Indian nation, the stories change, sometimes subtly, sometimes quite drastically, and no one singular view prevails.[21]

Ramanujan's essay irritated Hindu activists precisely because it showed that there is no one, unique rendering or interpretation of the Ramayana. Not surprisingly, the student activists called it 'malicious, capricious, fallacious, and offensive to the beliefs of millions of Hindus'.[22]

But to silence a voice that says that
there are many versions of Ramayana is not
only an act of crude censorship and an attack on Hindu intellect, it also goes against
the central tenet of Hinduism. The doyen
of Indian history, Romila Thapar, herself a
target of vicious attacks by Hindu nationalists, has shown how the Ramayana's many
versions embed stories reflecting social as-
pirations and ideological concerns of each
group that propounded a different version.
The Hindu nationalists' challenge to the diversity of voices is more a political proposi-
tion than a religious assertion.

And how diverse those narratives are—
not only across India, but as far away as In-
donesia, Thailand, Malaysia, Cambodia and
Laos where they vary even more widely
than in India. These multiple narratives in-
terfere with the master version of a strong,
virile, masculine and martial lord/warrior-
king—like the image now reinforced by Vir-

gin Comics in India which casts him as a muscular, Superman-like hero in *Ramayana 3392 AD*—that the BJP wants to project in India.

There is political purpose behind depicting Rama as a soldier, and not as *maryada purushottam* (the ideal man who knows his own and society's limits, and who will sacrifice his interests for others). And that is to inject militancy into the Hindus, who, the BJP believes, have been made to feel like second-class citizens in their own country. In her thought-provoking work on Hindu nationalism, US academic Martha Nussbaum observes:

> Hindu traditions emphasize tolerance and pluralism . . . But the traditions contain a wound, a locus of vulnerability, in the area of humiliated masculinity. For centuries, some Hindu males think, they were subordinated by a sequence of conquerors, and Hindus have come to iden-

Cover of Ramayana 3392 AD *by Virgin Comics.*

tify the sexual playfulness and sensuousness of their traditions . . . with their own
weakness. So a repudiation of the sensu-
ous and the cultivation of the masculine
came to be seen as the best way out.[23]

Feminist scholars are indeed appalled
by the Ramayana's overt masculinity. But
they have also found in Sita a cliché-ridden
representation of femininity, a docile
woman willing to be led whcrever her husband takes her and unquestioningly accepting her fate, including cruel punishments
and chastity tests. Gauri Parimoo Krishnan
notes: 'Valmiki's *Ramayana* has been
wrongly ascribed canonical status, giving
rise to a sort of patriarchal, literate, pan-In-
dian elitism which in recent times has been
scorned.'[24] In the Indian feminist magazine, *Manushi*, Nabaneeta Dev Sen and
Madhu Kishwar have written powerful cri-
tiques of the masculine interpretation of the
Ramayana.

A survey of Hindu epics may suggest that Hindu gods don't claim to be morally perfect; they do practise subterfuge and trickery. In an uncertain universe, we often have to act in ways that seem morally impure in order to achieve a higher end. That, indeed, is the message of the Mahabharata. On the other hand, the Ramayana aims to show how it is possible to lead a morally pure life. Rama's heroism is not simply based on his battlefield skills but also on his ability to place the interests of others—and his own sense of obligation—above his own.

Such sacrificial acts are passé; the BJP wants to project Rama as a superman. However, elevating him over other gods makes Hinduism seem monotheistic, a bit less like itself and a bit more like Islam or Christianity. The late Morarji Desai, a former Prime Minister, astutely noted this point in a conversation with me in the late-1980s, when the BJP was still only beginning to embark

on what then seemed like a quixotic campaign—to reclaim the site of the Babri
Masjid. 'They are playing a dangerous
game,' he told me. 'They want to create a
cult of Rama. They are converting Hinduism into Islam—they are making Hinduism a religion with one book
(Ramayana), one place of worship (Ayodhya) and one God (Rama). That is not Hinduism. Hinduism is about plurality.' It is a
point that even Arun Shourie, now a BJP
politician and a former economist and editor, agrees with.[25] This does not mean other
faiths are inferior or not inclusive; rather,
that contemporary thinkers who have written about Hinduism see polytheistic plural-
ism as its distinct characteristic.

THE RIGHT TO TAKE OFFENCE

One of the more curious outcomes of the
Salman Rushdie affair has been the idea

that, in the name of multiculturalism, society should not only accommodate the offended but also impose some curbs on free speech for fear of offending minorities. Now Hindus, the majority in India, want equal opportunity to be offended. This strategy has been successful because the Indian state stoops when asked, and fails to conquer. Hindu nationalists have intimidated critics physically, targeted academics outside India, research institutions at home and even editors expressing an opinion that upsets a particular political point of view.

Within months of the attack on the Ramanujan essay, in early November, ABVP's activists struck again at Delhi University, disrupting a seminar on communalism and fascism, where S. A. R. Geelani was to speak. Geelani is a Muslim who was acquitted in a case the government filed against those suspected of carrying out an attack on the Indian Parliament in 2001.

But the streak of intolerance is most pronounced in Maharashtra. This state has old ties with Hindu nationalism and was home to the first three leaders of the RSS— Keshav Baliram Hedgewar, Madhav Sadashiv Golwalkar and Madhukar Datta- traya Deoras. In his book *We, or Our Nation Defined*, Golwalkar praised the Aryan na- tionalism of Nazi Germany,[26] and admired the spirit of Adolf Hitler. B. J. Munje, an RSS activist, spent time in Italy in 1934 in awe of Benito Mussolini's fascist black- shirts.[27] Vinayak Damodar Savarkar, a free- dom fighter who spent years in the Cellular Jail in the Andamans, was a leader of the Hindu Maha Sabha (HMS). And Nathuram Godse, the man who assassinated Gandhi, was its member.

While the BJP's strength has been pri- marily in northern and central India, the Shiv Sena has been more powerful in Maha- rashtra. In the mid-1980s, the latter forged an alliance with the BJP, promoting the concept of *Hindutva*. The RSS has always been popular in Maharashtra, and most Marathi children grow up listening to hair-raising tales of the valiant Shivaji fighting Muslim warlords. An early example of Hindu nationalists and Marathi chauvinists opposing a work of art was the campaign against the late Vijay Tendulkar's remark-able play, *Ghashiram Kotwal*, which exposed the moral degeneracy of the rule of the Peshwas in Pune who ruled large parts of Maharashtra and beyond, from 1749 to 1818.

When it was invited to the Berlin The-atre Festival in 1982 and later to the UK, Hindu activists picketed the play, and the Theatre Academy of Pune could leave only after promising to the court that it would read a statement before each performance, saying that the play was a work of fiction and did not intend to denigrate the Peshwa rule or Chitpavan Brahmans, the community that claimed to have been offended.

India was going through an angst-ridden mid-life crisis at that time, the roots of which lay in the 1975 Emergency when, after an adverse court ruling that unseated her from Parliament, Prime Minister Indira Gandhi jailed opponents and suspended parts of the Constitution. The ease with which she could do this stunned many. Writing in *India: A Wounded Civilization* (1977), V. S. Naipaul saw, in the declaration of the Emergency, evidence of Indian institutions—the Press, the Parliament and the Judiciary—having been essentially borrowed. Mrs Gandhi lost the election that followed, but internal bickering among her successors disillusioned voters further.

The late-1970s witnessed insurgencies in Punjab, where the Sikhs were demanding a separate nation called Khalistan; and in Assam, where there was a movement

against foreigners, or Bangladeshi immigrants. Kashmir was once again in strife. In
June 1984, Mrs Gandhi launched Operation
Blue Star and sent the Indian Army into the
Golden Temple—the holiest shrine of the
Sikhs—to flush out Sikh terrorists who were
using the temple as their base. Many of them
died inside the temple. In retaliation, on 31
October 1984, she was assassinated by Beant
Singh and Satwant Singh, her bodyguards. In
the riots that followed, nearly 3,000 Sikhs,
mainly in northern India, were killed by
goons directed by Congress leaders. Mrs
Gandhi's son Rajiv Gandhi took over as
India's Prime   Minister and won a resound-
ing victory in parliamentary elections in December 1984. The Congress won over 400
seats out of 543 for the first time in history;
the BJP won two.

By 1987, cracks emerged in India's old
order. India had professed non-alignment,
but had essentially cast its lot with the Soviet
bloc, and its economy had a mutually advan-

tageous barter arrangement with many Soviet bloc states. With Mikhail Gorbachev's
perestroika (restructuring) and *glasnost*
(openness), things began to change. And as
the Soviet satellite states began to assert
their independence, India saw its market
share decline. Could the reliance on a so-
cialist model of economic planning survive?
India had already begun to attract invest-
ments in hi-tech industries. Just as social-
ism seemed to fray, so did non-alignment.
As the Soviet bloc crumbled, the second
tenet of Nehruvian governance, non-alignment, appeared meaningless. What was
India aligned against, except the US, in the
post-Soviet world?

And that made some people begin to
question the third tenet of Nehru's governing philosophy—secularism. This did not
emerge out of a vacuum: to understand
this, think of the Shah Bano case, a lawsuit
in which Shah Bano, a 58-year-old woman,
sued her husband, seeking maintenance

under India's divorce laws. The husband declined—under Islamic law he had already given the *mehr* (alimony) and now owed her nothing. The case reached the Supreme Court, which ruled in her favour, saying she could not be denied her rights as an Indian citizen.

Leaders representing the Muslim community revolted; they campaigned vigorously against the judgement, arguing that the verdict attacked Islam. Chief Justice Yashwant Vishnu Chandrachud did not help matters by making remarks, partly in jest, about the Quran. Instead of drawing on his huge parliamentary support, Rajiv Gandhi succumbed, and passed a law that effectively denied Muslim women access to courts to challenge inequitable rulings under the Muslim personal law.

Now it was the turn of many secular, liberal Indians, including, of course, many liberal Muslims, to be stunned. Newspapers wrote editorials criticizing the state, but the only politicians who vigorously opposed the Gandhi administration were from the BJP. Its leaders shrewdly—and correctly—estimated that this was their golden opportunity to win support among the outwardly secular, well-educated, urban, middle-class Hindus. They were not to be disappointed: within two years, the Gandhi administration scored another spectacular own goal.

By mid-1987, the word was out that Rushdie had written a novel about angels and devils, that it dealt with the birth of a great religion and was supposed to be a literary masterpiece. *The Satanic Verses* was published in 1988, but the publisher's consulting editor for India, Khushwant Singh, warned Penguin not to publish it—it would certainly cause riots across India, if not beyond. Singh may have shown prescience but he failed to uphold freedom of expression. Penguin did not release the book in India, and the government prevented its import into the country. *India Today,* which had published the excerpts that brought attention to the novel, criticized the decision in an editorial. To paraphrase Benjamin Franklin, India had chosen safety over liberty and had ceased to deserve either.

On 14 February 1989, Ayatollah Khomeini, the supreme leader of the Iranian revolution, imposed a *fatwa* on Rushdie that decreed his death for the insults he had heaped upon Prophet Mohammed. Rushdie went into hiding; protests followed in India, and several dozen people died. Singh had been proved right, but, as India had already decided to ban the book, by then his prophecy was, at one level, meaningless. The riots would have occurred any way.

What shocked many at that time was the speed with which the Indian government had banned the novel. Following the

fatwa, the novel was burned in Bradford
and the idea of the right to be offended got
firmly established. In India, many communities—even professions—began to demand
bans on what they did not like. In 1989, a
businessman wanted a film called *Tamas*
(Darkness) to be banned because he feared
it would ignite tensions between Hindus
and Muslims. Around the same time, Shiv
Sena activists humiliated playwright Iqbal
Khwaja, who had written a funny play
called *Shakespeare ke Ram-Leela*, (Shakespeare's tales told using the idiom of Ramayana) because they claimed it offended
them. Lawyers protested against a film, *New
Delhi Times* (1986), in which a journalist tells
his wife, a lawyer, that all lawyers are liars.
Earlier, the police did not like their representation in the realistic film, *Ardh-Satya*
(*Half-truth*, 1983). And Christians said they
wanted a play in Malayalam, *Christuvite
Aram Thirumurivu* (The Sixth Holy Wound

of Christ)[28] banned, as it was based on the Nikos Kazantzakis play *The Last Temptation of Christ.* Maharashtra Navnirman Sena (Maharashtra Rebuilding Army), founded by Shiv Sena-founder Bal Thackeray's nephew, Raj, recently managed to get a popular sweetshop in Bombay to change its name from Karachi Sweet Mart to Jai Sri Krishna Sweet Mart, because Karachi is in Pakistan, from where the sweet shop's Hindu owners had come as refugees at the time of the Partition.

In recent years, just as the Shiv Sena launched its campaign against Valentine's Day, a Bombay academic, Pratibha Naithani, formed Ashlilta Virodh Manch (Forum Against Obscenity) and run vigorous campaigns against films, TV shows, billboards and advertisements which, in her view, are obscene. Her success is at least partly because the Shiv Sena's protests have made acquiescence necessary. Liberal, femi-

nist academics and journalists, who oppose
images that portray women as sex objects,
have also campaigned on this theme.

The Hindu nationalist argument,
couched in the language of equality, was
that if others can get things banned, why
can't Hindus? And it initiated its campaign
to restore Hindu pride. Posters began to appear everywhere, urging Hindus to feel
proud of their faith. *'Garv se kaho, ham
Hindu hai'* (Say with pride, I am a Hindu)
the slogans said, and state-run television
began to show a privately-made serial
telling the story of Ramayana. Made by Ra-
manand Sagar, a Bollywood director, the serial had poor visual effects, acting and
dialogue, but it was syrupy-sweet and full of
homilies, and contributed significantly in
developing the cult of Rama, even spawn-
ing lucrative businesses. While the movement to build the Rama temple in Ayodhya
was never due to one specific cause, it is fair

to say that Sagar's Ramayana created an environment in which a mass movement to honour Rama became possible and the RSS dream seemed closer to reality.[29]

And it was in that environment that Lal Krishna Advani, later to become India's Deputy Prime Minister, discovered the joys of travelling in a Toyota truck. The destination: Ayodhya. The claim: that the Babri Masjid, built by Babar, the first Mughal emperor who ruled India from 1526 to 1530, must be replaced by a grand temple for Rama. The mosque stood in the way of the chariot; it had to make way.

The campaign to reclaim the mosque was a high-risk strategy the BJP undertook in an attempt to come to power on its terms by flaunting its Hindu nationalist credentials. Rajiv Gandhi lost the 1989 elections, and, two short-lived coalitions later, in 1991, while on the comeback trail, a suicide bomber assassinated him at an election

6 December 1992: members of a frenzied mob atop the Babri Masjid.

rally. The Congress limped back to power, but, in December 1992, the Babri Masjid was razed.

FAILURE OF AN IDEAL

The destruction of the mosque was a deep blow to Indian secularism. If assassination is a form of censorship, the mosque destruction was the metaphorical equivalent of destroying a culture, an identity. There was nothing spectacular about Babri Masjid; India has grander, more beautiful mosques. But it was unique because it stood in the town many believe to be Rama's birthplace and because of the perception that Babar's invading army had destroyed a temple there. The dispute simmered for decades, but a court order soon after Independence prevented either side from disturbing the site. Through the 1980s, the Vishwa Hindu Parishad (VHP; World Hindu Council) had made progressively louder noises seeking to reclaim the site. Muslims had formed the Babri Masjid Action Committee and refused to surrender their claim. Angry Hindus formed the Rama Janambhoomi (birthplace) liberation movement.

On 6 December 1992, Advani sat watching a frenzied mob he had encouraged first climb atop the mosque and then raze it, all in a little more than four hours. '*Ek dhakka aur do, masjid ko tod do*' (One more push, and destroy the mosque), screamed Sadhvi Ritambhara, a Hindu priestess, cheering the crowds. Many Hindus saw redemption in that destruction.

In the years since, despite the BJP having been in power for six years, the promised grand temple hasn't been built at the spot. Hindu activists have periodically turned up in Ayodhya, threatening to start construction, only to retreat after a fresh court order. When one such group of Hindu activists was returning from Ayodhya in February 2002, their railway compartment caught fire in a town called Godhra in Gujarat. Many believe the fire was started by a Muslim mob, although the evidence is mixed. Some 58 people, most of them Hindu activists, died in that fire. Hindus in Gujarat, where the BJP rules, retaliated swiftly, killing hundreds of Muslims, shattering Muslim shrines, looting property and displacing thousands of Muslim families. Capitalizing on the riots, Narendra Modi, Gujarat's Chief Minister, dissolved the legislature and sought fresh elections. Many, including Human Rights Watch, have accused him of complicity in the pogrom. He has, however, been re-elected twice.

Gujarat is the laboratory of Hindu nationalists, complained progressive Indians. The VHP agreed, promising a repeat of Gujarat if Muslims dared misbehave elsewhere in India. After winning elections in Karnataka, its Chief Minister said he wanted to emulate Modi. Such talk and violence, reminiscent of the months leading up to India's Partition, is once again part of India's discourse. And its success is because India's secular model has failed.

For Hindu nationalists—who aim at reclaiming and rewriting history—the Babri Masjid was the symbol of historic subjugation. Besides Ayodhya, they are interested in restoring temples in Kashi and Mathura. Some nationalists have listed thousands of temples that were destroyed, seeking retribution of some kind.

The aim of the destruction in Ayodhya was to insist that there was one prevailing view of how Indian society was to be structured, and Hinduism, as defined by Hindu nationalists, would dictate that national narrative. Indeed, Nobel Laureate V. S. Naipaul, who sees the rise of Hindu nationalism as a positive development, called the

mosque destruction 'an inevitable retribution'. But placing the act in its historical
context, Indian historian Romila Thapar
told me: 'The demolition of the mosque
was a violent, aggressive act of destruction
claiming to glorify Hinduism but was a far
cry from representing civilized Hindu val-
ues.' She also said:

> This fallacious idea that the past can be
> changed through destroying the surviv-
> ing heritage from the past was a blatant
> attack on history: for the axiom of history
> is that the past cannot be changed, but
> that if we intelligently understand the
> past, then the present and the future can
> be changed. The destruction of the her-
> itage of a society, as also happened in the
> case of the Taliban destroying the images
> of the Buddha at Bamiyan, is the subordi-
> nation of past history to present politics.[30]

Academics who identify such complexi-
ties are the natural, next target. And that
battle has become global.

THE LONG ARM OF FUNDAMENTALISM

Paul Courtright teaches religion at Emory University in Atlanta, and is an expert on Ganesha, the elephant-headed Hindu god. In 1985, he published a book[31] that explored Oedipal overtones in Ganesha's story—Ganesha was willing to fight his father, Shiva, God of Destruction, to protect his mother, Parvati. In the ensuing conflict, Shiva, who did not know Ganesha was his son because he had been away for a long time, beheaded him. When a horrified Parvati told him whom he had killed, he replaced Ganesha's head with the head of the nearest creature he could find, an elephant. Courtright was also intrigued by the phallic symbolism of the elephant's trunk. Drawing on the story of a conflict between a woman's husband and son, he suggested that Shiva had chosen an elephant's head because the trunk represented a limp phallus. By contrast, he said, Shiva's power is represented in idols by a *linga*—an erect phallus.

For nearly two decades, few people other than academics had heard about Courtright's book. But, in 2004, some Hindu nationalists launched a spirited campaign against him on the Internet. Within days, Courtright received death threats. A petition signed by thousands of Hindus in the US read: 'We find it deeply offensive and repulsive to our innermost sensibilities that a member of Emory's faculty should use "psychoanalysis" for interpreting sacred symbols of Hinduism in an erotic manner.' Others challenged the religious origins of Western professors writing about Hinduism, asking why Protestant, Methodist or Baptist academics were interpreting Hinduism. Later that year, at a public lecture in London, Wendy Doniger, who teaches the history of religion at the University of Chicago and who has written 20 books about India and Hinduism, had an egg flung at her. The attacker missed the target. The same year,

Macalester College religious studies professor James W. Laine's book on Shivaji[32] provoked anger and attacks. One of his Indian associates, Shrikant Bahulkar, was physically assaulted—tar was applied to his face, a particularly egregious form of insult in India—and the renowned Bhandarkar Oriental Research Institute, where Laine did some of his primary research, was vandalized and rare manuscripts destroyed. BJP Prime Minister Atal Behari Vajpayee told Laine not to 'play with our national pride'.

Critics of these scholars zeroed in on what they called 'inaccuracies' in scholarly research, asserting that these errors negated the body of their work. In an interview with the *Washington Post*, Doniger said: 'The argument is being fuelled by a fanatical nationalism and *Hindutva*, which says no one has the right to make a mistake, and no one who is not a Hindu has the right to speak about Hinduism at all.'[33]

The man at the centre of these campaigns is a New Jersey-based telecommuni-
cations specialist called Rajiv Malhotra, who
has since set up The Infinity Foundation
that seeks to remove 'whiteness' from the
study of India by Westerners, and who has
been funding academics sympathetic to
Hindu nationalism to rewrite Indian history
from an Indian nationalist perspective,
which appears similar to a Hindu perspective although Malhotra insists he is not a
Hindu nationalist. In one of his early inter-
ventions on a website, Malhotra wrote that
academics like Doniger and her many students had 'erotised and denigrated Hinduism' which led to Americans
misunderstanding India. Malhotra was particularly incensed by Courtright's book, for
which Doniger had written the foreword.

There were many protests after Malhotra's essay appeared on the website, and a
group of Hindus sought a meeting with the

President of Emory University, seeking Courtright's dismissal. T. R. N. Rao, a professor of computer science at the University of Lousiana at Lafayette, initiated an Internet petition against the book and got some 7,000 signatures within one week; many of the posts threatened violence against Courtright. Rao removed the petition when he saw the violent threats. To critics who said that using psychoanalytical scholarship to explore the sexual motivations or fantasies of Gods was wrong, Courtright replied, 'The Hindu tradition talks about sex a lot, especially in the contexts of marriage and asceticism. In [Ganesha's] story, very important, useful, ancient and generalizable insights about human life, desire, and sexuality are being offered to us.'

The book's publisher, Oxford University Press, withdrew the book in India. Hindus in the US then notched up another success: following a campaign started by

Sankrant Sanu, an activist who was at one time an engineer at Microsoft, they got Microsoft's Encarta encyclopaedia to replace an essay on Hinduism written by Doniger with one by Arvind Sharma, who teaches comparative religion at McGill University in Canada. Sanu's objection: insiders interpret every other faith in the US but Hinduism is the only one that has been consistently interpreted by Western academics. Emboldened by Sanu's rhetoric, one Internet blog-post said, 'Hindus worldwide (except so far in India) are shocked at how Protestant-dominated pedagogues in academia caricature Hinduism as part of proselytising, and then stifle discussion.'

Laine had a different set of problems. He was writing about a seventeenth-century Hindu king revered in Maharashtra. His book on Shivaji implied that Shivaji's parents may have been estranged. In retaliation, the Sambhaji Brigade, a pro-Hindu group, destroyed manuscripts at the Bhandarkar Institute in Pune. As an academic, Laine admits there are different ways of interpreting the past. In an interview with the Indian magazine *Tehelka*, he argues, 'I am not interested in whether this or that element is "true" but in the motivations writers have to nudge the story this way or that.' Part of legitimate query in the life of a historian, but dangerous when you are dealing with uninformed foot soldiers of *Hindutva*.

Questioning anything about Shivaji is a difficult business in Maharashtra. The attacks continue. When Kumar Ketkar, Editor, *Loksatta*, a Marathi daily, wrote recently questioning the wisdom of building a gigantic statue commemorating Shivaji on India's West Coast, supporters of Shivaji surrounded his house, attacked it, destroyed his personal property but left him unharmed. For good measure, Ketkar translated his article into English, and *Loksatta*'s sister publication,

Indian Express, published it.[34] International PEN has adopted Ketkar as a writer under threat.

Doniger is concerned by such attacks. She told the *Washington Post* interviewer in an e-mail, 'Malhotra's ignorant writings have stirred up more passionate emotions in Internet subscribers who know even less than Malhotra does, who do not read books at all, and these people have reacted with violence. I therefore hold him indirectly responsible.' Malhotra, for his part, has condemned the attackers as 'hooligans'.

Malhotra has been writing at length on his views of US academia and says he was inspired by the stance taken by African-American scholars at Princeton University, who challenged the white view of the world during the Civil Rights Movement there. The *Washington Post* article I have cited earlier has him saying: 'In the US, everything is negotiable—you have to negotiate who you are and how they think of you.' His foundation claims to work towards upgrading 'the portrayal of India's civilization in the American education system and media'. But as Vijay Prashad, a historian who teaches at Trinity College in Hartford, Connecticut, argues, marketing a nation is not the responsibility of academics; ambassadors are paid to do that.

But Hindus in the US have been particularly restless. They have now taken their protests beyond academia and into popular culture. Rajan Zed, the first Hindu priest to be invited to pray at the US Congress in July 2007, recently led a campaign against the comedy film *Love Guru*, saying it denigrated Hinduism. This came on top of several similar protests over other perceived slights against Hinduism. Other acts that offended them included Stanley Kubrick's film *Eyes Wide Shut* (1999), in which Sanskrit chants from the *Bhagavadgita* are recited during a sexual orgy. Mahadev Sheziyan, a Hindu in the US, wrote on an Internet chat-group:

> Hindus are perceived as meek and the world knows they will not complain, so anything goes. Had Hindus been bombing World Trade Centers (I am saying this only to contrast, and I do not advocate harming any civilian target), these idiots wouldn't have taken such liberties with the *Gita*.

Another protestor ranted:

> The defaced Shiva *Lingas* at Hinglaj (Baluchistan) and Peshawar, the universities at Takshshila and Nalanda, thousands of demolished temples scattered all over India, are mute witnesses to the complacency of our own ancestors who once thought along the same lines, that Hinduism does not need any defence. There is no philosophical difference between a Mahmud Ghazni demolishing Somanath [a temple in western India] and a Kubrick

defiling *Gita shlokas* [verses] in his third-rate movie.

It takes little to offend Hindus now. When rock star Madonna sported a *bindi* (dot on the forehead) there were protests. Other acts that angered Hindus include the rock group Aerosmith's release of a CD whose jacket showed Krishna with the face of a cat and the breasts of a woman; the scantily clad Xena's call on Krishna to help her tame her rivals in *Xena: The Warrior Princess*; and Mike Myers' pose as Goddess Kali, with blue-skinned, bare-breasted buxom women lying around him wearing robes, *mehendi* (henna applied on the palm) and *bindi*.[35] An Indian consultant in the US told me when I wrote about the controversy, 'The same artists would think real hard before causing offence to any of the Semitic religions [Judaism, Christianity or Islam], but nobody is scared of a Hindu backlash.' Aerosmith, Sony, who released the CD, and photographer David Chappelle, who took the Myers photograph, promptly apologized to the Hindus. Nina Paley, a New York-based filmmaker who has made a charming, award-winning animation film called *Sita Sings the Blues*, in which she compares her life to Sita's, has been attacked on various websites. Recently, a Hindu group protested when PBS announced it would show the film.

But in terms of *chutzpah*, few campaigns are as significant as the one that took on the appointment of Thapar, easily India's most distinguished historian, to the Kluge Chair for the Countries and Cultures of the South at the US Library of Congress. Widely acclaimed for her scholarship on ancient India, 77-year-old Thapar has been fighting a spirited battle against Hindu nationalists, arguing for academic freedom and the spirit of open inquiry in India. When the Library of Congress appointed her in 2003, the campaign against her was at once vicious and vacuous. Calling her appointment 'a great travesty', the petitioners collected thousands of signatures online. She was called 'an avowed antagonist' of Hindu civilization and a Marxist who has discredited Hindus and accused of engaging in 'a war of cultural genocide'.

Appropriately enough, in December 2008, Thapar was jointly awarded the John W. Kluge Prize, a Library of Congress achievement award for the study of the humanities. She was honoured for work showing Indian civilization as more pluralistic than was widely accepted. Hindu activists don't like Thapar because she grounds her work in methods of historical investigation that are peer-reviewed and she goes as far as the facts take her; she does not modify facts to suit theories. Her disagreement with Hindu activists may seem academic, but their attempt to silence her is part of the BJP's project of remaking India. Like many scholars, Thapar uses some Marxist categories of historiography; she is attacked not for her scholarship, but for her politics. The evidence Thapar provides complicates the BJP's simple narrative. Why would a septuagenarian historian evoke so much passion that Hindu nationalists want to silence her? To understand that, let us turn to the Hindu nationalists' quest to take over Indian history.

HISTORY FOR THE TAKING

The central tenet of *Hindutva* says India must recapture its proud past. The world owes India its place at the centre of human civilization. If the world won't acknowledge it, India will seek attention by doing something spectacular, such as going nuclear—as it did, first in 1974 and again, as a reminder, in 1998. Islamic invasions and the colonial period may have hurt the Hindu psyche, but India is now ready for the big league. It has arrived—no longer whining or pining but shining.

The BJP wants that outcome, and its leaders want to transform the way Indians think over a generation or two. Hence, the focus on history. Change how Indians perceive their past, and then shape the future. Wipe out the inconvenient parts, and reinforce myths. The BJP wants to demonstrate that Indian history, as written by 'leftist' Indian historians such as Thapar, Dwijendra Narayan Jha—who has shown that there was no taboo against eating beef among Hindus—and Bipan Chandra, is distorted.

It is, of course, true that some leftist historians[36] have overlooked Communist collaboration with the British during the freedom struggle, as well as underplayed Stalin's massacres in the Soviet Union, Mao's follies in China and the destruction

of Hindu temples by Muslim rulers. But
what have today's Muslims got to do with
what some invader did centuries ago? Yet,
invoking the ghosts of the past, or 'ancient
hatreds', is a time-honoured technique
demagogues have deployed to effect.

In India, the leader of the campaign
against historians during the years of BJP
rule was the then Minister for Human Re-
source Development, Science and Technology, Murli Manohar Joshi. He oversaw
efforts to rewrite history textbooks, to reflect more accurately the pain caused to
Hindu civilization by invading foreigners,
usually Muslims. To be sure, rewriting history is often necessary, as in the case of
modern Japan. Successive Japanese governments have avoided educating Japanese
children about the horrors the Imperial
Japanese Army inflicted upon East Asia between the 1930s and 1940s. Those seeking
to rewrite Japanese history want to inject re-

morse and humility. Joshi's intention seeks
the reverse: to make Hindus more aggressive and proud by reminding Muslims that
they must be subservient and apologize for
the past. By stressing the atrocities that
Muslims committed and erasing the shared
past—of sitar and samosas, for instance—
the BJP's historians may not make Hindus
feel any prouder, but they would certainly
make Indian Muslims insecure. In the history promoted by the BJP, Islam and
Sikhism don't merit a mention in a chapter
on major religions for Class IX; other texts
don't say that India's founding father, Mohandas Karamchand Gandhi, was assassinated by a Hindu fanatic.

The BJP's first step was to withdraw history books that interfered with the project.
The foot soldiers then attacked research institutions and destroyed reputations in pur-
suit of a situation where minorities know
their place in a Hindu-dominated India—

the exact reverse of the kind of India that Gandhi envisioned.

In this quest, the first target is the esoteric Aryan Invasion Theory, the building block of Indian history. Conventional history says that, around 5,000 years ago, the Aryans came to India as immigrants or invaders and settled around the Indus Valley, creating the Mohenjodaro and Harappa civilization. There is no single explanation of who came and from where, but we know that there was contact with others who lived there, known as Dravidians. Over centuries, groups intermingled, creating the complex Indian society. Islam and Christianity came to India much later, leading to the multi-everything Indian identity of today.

Accepting this scenario requires recognition of the holistic, inclusive and syncretic nature of Indian society, a rich amalgam of many influences and ethnicities. But you can challenge that view by providing an

alternative, ethnically pure one that holds
that there was no Aryan invasion. According
to the revisionists, Hindu civilization pre-
dated everything, and India had always
been the land of *sanatana dharma* (eternal
faith). Invasions, if any, only occurred in the
last millennium, first by Islamic invaders
who looted temples and killed thousands,
and, later, during the colonial period. As
Thapar observes:

> For those concerned with a *Hindutva* ide-
> ology, the [Aryan] invasion had to be de-
> nied. The definition of a Hindu as given
> by Savarkar was that India had to be his
> *pitrubhumi* [fatherland] and his *punyab-
> humi* [the land of his faith]. A Hindu
> could not be descended from alien in-
> vaders. Since Hindus sought a lineal de-
> scent from the Aryans, and a cultural
> heritage, the Aryans had to be indige-
> nous. This definition of the Hindu ex-
> cluded Muslims and Christians from
> being indigenous, since their religion
> did not originate in India.[37]

That is the political import of the exercise: that Muslims and Christians in India are foreigners. This is no longer an impenetrable debate among Indologists, but a vigorous argument that goes to the heart of the Indian identity.

Interestingly, the charges against these academics are not led by historians. Writers who oppose the historians include David Frawley, a US Ayurvedic doctor; Koenraad Elst, a Belgian Hindu philosopher; N. S. Rajaram, a former consultant with NASA; Bhagwan Gidwani, a retired tourism official; and Shrikant Talageri, a former bank officer. They have made a virtue of the necessity: their not being historians is precisely the point. They claim that contemporary history and archaeology departments in universities have become a cartel of historians agreeing with one another; these academics have reputations to protect. By challenging their orthodoxy, these maverick 'historians' intend to reclaim India's genuine past.

While Elst, Frawley, Rajaram and others continue to write voluminously, few historians have taken their work seriously. Michael Witzel, Professor of Indology, Harvard University, has called their attempts guesswork, and believes that their decipherment of Indus script is based on an incredibly flexible Indus 'alphabet' and compounded and bolstered by actual fraud.[38] As an example, Witzel cites Rajaram's effort to prove horses existed in pre-historic India. Why this obsession with the horse? We know from zoology and archaeology that there were no horses in India till early in the second millennium BC. But if Rajaram can show that there were horses in India before the Indus civilization (BC 2600–1900), then he can presumably 'prove' that the *Rig Veda* preceded the Indus civilization. Why? Because the *Rig Veda* refers to horses. The existence

of horses would, Rajaram and his col-
leagues hope, disprove the commonly accepted theory that the speakers of
Indo-Aryan languages came from outside
on horses. Witzel concludes: 'Apparently,
they do not realise how ridiculous all of this
reads outside the confines of the revisionists' rewriting of Indian history along au-
tochthonous lines. Their claims are
historically impossible and are based on an
unsubstantiated reading of the script.'[39] But
Witzel, the nationalists argue, is a West-
erner, with an imperial history and reputa-
tion to defend.

After 'establishing' that India was always a Hindu civilization, their next target
is Islamic invasion. Blaming historians affil-
iated to Jawaharlal Nehru University in
Delhi for understating the horrors of Muslim rule in India, the revisionists quote Per-
sian scholar Al-Biruni, and Gulbadan,
Babar's daughter, talking about Islamic

rulers taking Hindu slaves and killing
Hindu women and children, and of how
Mahmud Ghazni became one of the richest
men in the world in AD 1000 because of the
number of Hindu slaves he commanded.

Islam, they then assert, is not a religion
of peace. Writers sympathetic to the RSS,
Sita Ram Goel for instance, have exten-
sively documented how Islamic invaders destroyed Hindu temples and killed
thousands. To set these historical wrongs
right, the Hindu activists say they don't
want to reclaim all the temples that were
destroyed, they only want Ayodhya, Kashi
and Mathura. Perhaps they should reflect
on an incident from the life of Hindu
thinker Swami Vivekananda, who looked
disconsolate when he learned of temples
destroyed by Muslim invaders in mediaeval
India. The Goddess is supposed to have
spoken to him at that time, and asked: 'Do
you need my protection, or do I need

yours?' Divinities, if they exist, are presumably strong enough to survive criticism: it is
us lesser mortals who are fundamentally in-
capable of handling criticism.

Temple destruction, the major basis of
Hindu complaints, needs to be seen in context. In Kashmir, Thapar has shown, whenever the Hindu kings faced a financial
crisis, they sent their troops to loot the temple and, if necessary, destroy it. The
eleventh-century King Harshadeva appointed officers in a category known as *deva
utpatana nayaka* (officer in charge of uprooting temples). As Thapar demonstrates, the
destruction of Hindu temples was by no
means a Muslim monopoly. Indeed, the
Parmar rulers of Malva went to war against
the Chalukyas, which led to the destruction
of Jain temples in Saurashtra. The king also
destroyed a mosque the Chalukyas had
built for Arab traders in Cambay: 'By destroying their temples and their mosque, he

was demonstrating to the local people of Gujarat that he was capable of destroying those who were the backbone of the economy of Gujarat. It is more than just religious iconoclasm.'[40] There are other examples—of a Rashtrakuta king fighting the Pratiharas and his elephants uprooting a temple's courtyard.

But that's not the conversation the Hindu nationalists want. They assert that India has failed to come to grips with its past because its mind has been colonized. The Congress leaders who led India's freedom movement—Gandhi, Vallabhbhai Patel, Nehru—were all educated in the UK. They were Anglicized and original Macaulayites, a reference to Thomas Macaulay, whose 1835 *Minute on Indian Education* led to the spread of English education in India. Today, Macaulay is known for two statements: that 'a single shelf of a good European library is worth the whole native literature of India and Arabia'; and that   imperial Britain should create 'a class who may be interpreters between us and the millions whom we govern; a class of persons, Indian in blood and colour, but English in taste, in opinions, in morals and in intellect.' The Hindu nationalists say that Macaulay's 'children', or India's English-educated elite—in which they bracket everyone they disagree with—could scarcely understand the reality of India, and must be blamed for all that has gone wrong with the country in its first 50 years of freedom.

The final target is Gandhi. While no BJP leader has openly questioned Gandhi, in the mood *Hindutva* has allowed, questioning of the orthodoxy around Gandhi has become permissible. Plays and films that show Gandhi in less hagiographic ways than in Richard Attenborough's film have become popular. No more than any divinity should Gandhi be immune from criticism—

he would be the first to deny any halo around his head. Indeed, one of the better effects of Attenborough's film is that other directors have taken complex personalities from the same period—Subhas Chandra Bose, Ambedkar, Patel and others—and made biographical films about their lives, enriching India's understanding of its past.

It is the political project behind *Hindutva*—the undermining of other faiths—that Thapar challenges. Speaking at a history conference in Thiruvananthapuram in 2000, she said:

> To comprehend the present and move towards the future requires an understanding of the past: an understanding that is sensitive, analytical and open to critical enquiry. Indian historians' writing in the last 50 years . . . were not only fine examples of historical enquiry but were also pointers to new ways of extending historical methods. They widened and sharp-

ened the intellectual foundations of the
discipline of history and enriched the understanding of the Indian nation. These
studies have now come under attack . . . It
is because of this assault on history that
some of us have to speak in defence of the
discipline of history.

By championing *Hindutva*, the BJP is
making Indians identify with a narrower
definition of the state. Its goal is not to win
only the next election, but also the next
generation. The rewriting of history and
the erasure of the past are not to cast fresh
light on the past, but to make particular
readings of history fit prevailing political
requirements. The *Hindutva* movement is
not concerned with what India was like; it
wants to shape what India will be like and
wants its version of Hinduism to play the
defining role. It means hiding inconvenient
truths, denigrating complex heroes that
muddle the narrative, simplifying the her-

itage and destroying or discrediting all those who stand in the way.

This stems from deep-rooted insecurity, not pride. India's greatest strength has been its openness to external influences. Foreigners who come to India get assimilated. India welcomes alien influences. It honours its artists—it does not hound them. It celebrates its diversity and does not feel threatened by people who think or feel differently. And while these are virtues of the modern Indian nation, they are rooted in that inclusive ethos, which at least coincides with Hinduism's liberal philosophy, even if not a product of it or influenced by it.

Gandhi talked of inclusive nationalism. Rabindranath Tagore, the Nobel Prize-winning poet who wrote the national anthems of India and Bangladesh, shunned the idea of borders; for him, the world was his nation. Gandhi admitted he could not be as broadminded as the poet; nonetheless, he said:

> I do not want my house to be walled in on all sides and my windows to be stuffed. I want the cultures of all the lands to be blown about my house as freely as possible. But I refuse to be blown off my feet by any.[41]

Not for him the cowardly way out of censoring ideas he found challenging. As for Tagore, he taught us something else. In a poem that could well be the anthem for free thought, he wrote:

> *Where the mind is without fear and the head is held high;*
> *Where knowledge is free;*
> *Where the world has not been broken up into fragments by narrow domestic walls;*
> *Where words come out from the depth of truth;*
> *Where tireless striving stretches its arms towards perfection;*
> *Where the clear stream of reason has not lost*

*its way into the dreary desert sand of dead
habit;*
*Where the mind is led forward by thee into
ever-widening thought and action—*
*Into that heaven of freedom, my Father, let my
country awake.*[42]

Whenever Hindu nationalists attack an
art gallery, or tear down posters they consider obscene, or demand bans on books
they don't want others to read, or vandalize
a research institute, or destroy the home of
an editor, or threaten an academic, or run a
campaign against a historian they disagree
with, or force film studios to change scripts,
alter lyrics, or extract apologies from artists,
or hurl eggs at scholars, or destroy
mosques, rape Muslim women or kill Muslim men and children, they take India into
a deeper abyss; they push Hinduism into a
darker age. They look and act like the Nazis
and the Taliban. They plunge their country
into an darkness, are untrue to the meaning of their faith and are disloyal to their

nation's Constitution. They shame a great
nation and belittle how Rushdie saw India:
'The dream we had all agreed to dream.'

Notes

1 Few writers have captured the harrowing
   reality as well as Saadat Hasan Manto.
   Good introductions to his works are Alok
   Bhalla, *Life and Works of Saadat Hasan
   Manto* (Hyderabad: Indian Institute of
   Advanced Studies, 1997); *The Life and
   Works of Saadat Hasan Manto* (introduc-
   tion Leslie Flemming; Tahira Naqvi
   trans.) (Lahore: Vanguard Books, 1985);
   and Leslie A. Flemming, *Another Lonely
   Voice: The Urdu Short Stories of Saadat
   Hasan Manto* (Berkeley: Centre for South
   and Southeast Asian Studies, University
   of California, 1979). Also see Khushwant
   Singh, *Train to Pakistan* (London: Chatto
   and Windus, 1956), a novel set during
   the Partition. For non-fiction accounts of

oral history, see Urvashi Butalia, *The Other Side of Silence: Voices from the Partition of India* (Durham: Duke University Press, 2000).

2   Salman Rushdie, *The Moor's Last Sigh* (London: Jonathan Cape, 1995).

3   Ibid., p. 376f.

4   Dom Moraes, *Bombay* (Time–Life International, 1979).

5   The Vedas (BC 1500—1000) are the oldest sacred texts of Hinduism. According to Hindu tradition, the Vedas were revealed orally by Divinity and hence are called *sruti* ('what is heard'). The Upanishads are Hindu scriptures, which speak of a spiritual and philosophical tradition that is concerned with the idea of self-realisation—a process by which one understands the ultimate nature of Reality (*brahman*). The *Bhagavadgita* ('Song of God') is considered one of the most important religious classics of the world. Part of the Mahabharata, this 700-verse poem comprise the conversation between Krishna

and Arjuna on the battlefield before the start of the Kurukshetra war.

6 'The law seeks to protect not those who protect themselves, but those whose prurient minds take delight and sexual pleasures from erotic writings'—Justices M. Hidayatullah, P. B. Gajendragadkar (CJ), K. N. Wanchoo, J. C. Shah and N. Rajagopala Ayyangar, 'Ranjit Udeshi vs State of Maharashtra' (Supreme Court of India, 19 August 1964). Available at: indiankanoon.org/doc/1623275/

7 Girja Kumar, *The Book on Trial: Fundamentalism and Censorship in India* (New Delhi: Har-Anand Publications, 1997), pp. 332–3.

8 Justice Sanjay Kishan Kaul, 'Maqbool Fida Husain vs Raj Kumar Pandey [Along With Crl. Revision Petition Nos. 280 And 282/2007]' (Delhi High Court, 8 May 2008). Also available at: indian kanoon.org/doc/1191397/

9 Ibid.

10 James Joyce, *A Portrait of The Artist as a Young Man* (New York: Penguin, 1992), pp. 268–9.

11 Reference to the film, *Gajagamini* (2000), which Husain directed, and in which Madhuri Dixit acted.

12 Suneet Chopra, 'Resist Colonial Thinking or See the Art Market Die', *The Financial Express* (14 May 2006).

13 M. F. Husain, in conversation with journalists, including author. 7–8 June 2008, Bonham's, London.

14 B. R. Mani, e-mail interview with author. 28 January 2009.

15 Partha Mitter, *Much-Maligned Monsters*: *History of European Reactions to Indian Art* (Chicago: University of Chicago Press, 1992).

16 B. R. Mani, e-mail interview with author. 28 January 2009.

17 Rita Banerji, *Sex and Power*: *Defining History, Shaping Societies* (Delhi: Penguin,

2008). The above quote is from an e-mail interview with author. 4 February 2009.

18 Eric Hobsbawm, 'Politics, Memory and the Revisions of History in the Twenty-first Century', Lecture delivered at Columbia University, 2003. Quoted in Subhash Gatade, 'Hating Romila Thapar', *Himal* (June 2003).

19 In Paula Richman (ed.), *Many Ramayanas: The Diversity of a Narrative Tradition in South Asia* (Berkeley: University of California Press, 1991), pp. 22–49.

20 Rama was a prince born to Queen Kaushalya and King Dasaratha of Ayodhya. On the eve of his coronation, Kaikeyi, another wife of Dasaratha, reminded him of an old promise he had made to her on the battlefield, and asked that her son, Bharata, be crowned king instead, and that Rama be exiled to the forest for 14 years. Rama left with his wife Sita and brother Lakshmana. In the

forest, the demon king of Lanka, Ravana, who coveted Sita, contrived to
abduct her. Rama assembled an army of
monkeys, attacked Lanka, killed Ravana,
liberated Sita, returned home to Ayodhya and claimed his rightful throne. One
night, surveying Ayodhya incognito, he
heard a washerman banishing his wife
when she returned to him after having
left him for another man. He told her he
was not Rama, who'd take back a woman
who had lived with another man. Deter-
mined to live by what he considered to
be the highest example, Rama expelled
Sita to the forest. Some years later, when
they met, and he was still uncertain
about the sincerity of her love for him,
Sita preferred to be swallowed by her
mother, Earth, instead of being sub-
jected to another humiliating test to
prove her purity and chastity.

21 Jonah Blank, *The Arrow of the Blue-Skinned
God: Retracing the Ramayana through India*
(New York: Grove Press, 2000).

22 For a report on the Ramanujan-essay controversy, see Raghu Karnad, 'Unlikely Arrows In Ram's Quiver', *Tehelka Magazine*, 5(10) (15 March 2008): 25–7.

23 Martha Nussbaum, Fears for Democracy in India, in *The Chronicle of Higher Education* (18 May 2007). Available at chronicle.com/weekly/v53/i37/37b00601.htm (subscribers only) and at www.cceia.org/resources/transcripts/5433.html. She expands on this theme in the chapter, 'Fantasies of Purity and Domination', in *The Clash Within*: *Democracy, Religious Violence, and India's Future* (Boston: Belknap Press, 2007), pp. 186–211.

24 Gauri Parimoo Krishnan, *Ramayana*: *A Living Tradition* (Singapore: National Museum of Singapore, 1996), p. 9, citing R. P. Goodman, in 'Yavat Sthasyanti Girayaha: The Adikavya and Legacy of Rsi Valmiki', Keynote address, Centenary of the Oriental Institute of the Maharaja Sayajirao University, Vadodara, 1996.

25 Arun Shourie, *Hinduism, Essence and Consequence: A Study of the Upanishads, the Gita, and the Brahma-Sutras* (Delhi: Vikas, 1980).

26 'Germany shocked the world by purging the country of the Semitic races—the Jews—in the highest manifestation of race. Germany has also shown how well nigh-impossible it is for races and cultures, having differences going to the root, to be assimilated into one united whole, a good lesson for us in Hindusthan to learn and profit by' (M. S. Golwalkar, *We, or Our Nationhood Defined*, Nagpur: Bharat Prakashan, 1939, p. 12).

27 His papers at the Nehru Memorial Library contain the following recorded statement ascribed to him: 'The Hindu *shastras* provide an adequate basis for the co-optation and stratification of all the Hindus of India. However, it can be implemented only when the reins of power in India are in the hands of some Hindu

dictator like Shivaji of the previous era or Mussolini or Hitler of the modern times. We have to make scientific plans for this and dedicate ourselves to its propagation' (Nehru Memorial Library Munje Papers, Microfilm Diary R.N.-2 193–36).

28 J. N. Darren Middleton (ed.), *Scandalizing Jesus? Kazantzakis's* The Last Temptation of Christ, *50 Years On* (London: Continuum, 2005) See, in particular, the chapter by Mini Chandran, 'Distant Flutter of a Butterfly: The Indian Response to the Last Temptation', pp. 135–44.

29 Arvind Rajagopal, *Politics after Television*: *Religious Nationalism and the Reshaping of the Indian Public* (Cambridge: Cambridge University Press, 2008).

30 Romila Thapar, Lecture delivered at Thiruvananthapuram, 2 March 2002. Published as 'India 2002: The Year That Was', *Seminar* 521 (January 2003).

31 Paul Courtright, *Ganesha: Lord of Obstacles, Lord of Beginning* (Oxford: Oxford University Press, 1985).

31 James W. Laine, *Shivaji: Hindu King in Islamic India* (Oxford: Oxford University Press, 2003).

33 In Shankar Vedantam, 'Wrath Over a Hindu God: U.S. Scholars' Writings Draw Threats From Faithful', *Washington Post* (10 April 2004).

34 Kumar Ketkar, 'All The Problems Have Been Solved; Now Let's Build A Statue', *Indian Express* (6 June 2008). Also available at: www.indianexpress.com/news/all-the-problems-have-been-solved.-now-lets-build-a-statue/319301

35 See Salil Tripathi, 'Enraged by Madonna and Nicole', *The New Statesman* (20 September 1999).

36 See, for example, Arun Shourie, *Eminent Historians: Their Technology, Their Line, Their Fraud* (Delhi: Harper Collins, 1999).

37 Romila Thapar, '*Hindutva* and History', *Frontline* 17(20) (30 September–13 October 2000). Also available at: www.hindu.com/fline/fl1720/17200150.htm

38 Michael Witzel and Steve Farmer, 'Horseplay in Harappa: The Indus Valley Decipherment Hoax', *Frontline*, 17(20) (30 September–13 October 2000).

39 Ibid.

40 Romila Thapar, in conversation with the author. January 2003, London.

41 *Young India* (1 June 1921): 170. For the full quotation, see, for example, Mahatma Gandhi, *All Men are Brothers: Autobiographical Reflections* (Krishna Kripalani, ed.) (London: Continuum International Publishing Group, 1980), pp. 142–3.

42 Rabindranath Tagore, 'Chitta Jethha Bhayshunya' ('Where the Mind is Without Fear'), in *Gitanjali* (Song Offerings) (Rabindranath Tagore trans.) (New York and London: The Macmillan Company, 1912).

INDEX
ON CENSORSHIP

Index on Censorship is Britain's leading organisation promoting freedom of expression. Our award-winning magazine and website provide a window for original, challenging and intelligent writing on this vital issue around the world. Our international projects in media, arts and education put our philosophy into action.

For information and enquiries go to www.indexoncensorship.org, or email enquiries@indexoncensorship.org